Author:
Jim Pipe studied Ancient & Modern History at the University of Oxford, then spent ten years in publishing before becoming a full-time writer. He has written numerous nonfiction books for children, many on historical subjects. He lives in Dublin, Ireland, with his lovely wife Melissa.

Artist:
David Antram was born in Brighton, England, in 1958. He studied at Eastbourne College of Art and then worked in advertising for fifteen years before becoming a full-time artist. He has illustrated many children's nonfiction books.

Series creator:
David Salariya was born in Dundee, Scotland. He has illustrated a wide range of books and has created and designed many new series for publishers in the U.K. and overseas. In 1989 he established The Salariya Book Company. He lives in Brighton with his wife, illustrator Shirley Willis, and their son Jonathan.

Editor: **Stephen Haynes**

Editorial Assistant: **Mark Williams**

© The Salariya Book Company Ltd MMVIII
No part of this publication may be reproduced in whole or in part, or stored in a retrieval system, or transmitted in any form or by any means, electronic, mechanical, photocopying, recording, or otherwise, without written permission of the publisher. For information regarding permission, write to Scholastic Inc., 557 Broadway, New York, NY 10012.

Published in Great Britain in 2008 by
The Salariya Book Company Ltd
25 Marlborough Place, Brighton BN1 1UB

ISBN-13: 978-0-531-13913-4 (lib. bdg.)   978-0-531-14854-9 (pbk.)
ISBN-10: 0-531-13913-1 (lib. bdg.)   0-531-14854-8 (pbk.)

All rights reserved.
Published in 2008 in the United States
by Franklin Watts
An imprint of Scholastic Inc.
Published simultaneously in Canada.

A CIP catalog record for this book is available from the Library of Congress.

Printed and bound in China.
Printed on paper from sustainable sources.

You Wouldn't Want to Sail on an Irish Famine Ship!

Written by
Jim Pipe

Illustrated by
David Antram

Created and designed by
David Salariya

A Trip Across the Atlantic You'd Rather Not Make

Franklin Watts
An Imprint of Scholastic Inc.
NEW YORK • TORONTO • LONDON • AUCKLAND • SYDNEY
MEXICO CITY • NEW DELHI • HONG KONG
DANBURY, CONNECTICUT

Contents

Introduction

You are Brian Walsh, a farmer living in the west of Ireland in the 1840s. It's hard work feeding your family and paying rent to your landlord, but Ireland is a peaceful and beautiful place. Then in 1845 everything changes. There have been famines before, but nothing like this. Year after year, a mystery disease wipes out your potato crop—your main source of food.

Your landlord lives in England. He's more worried about the rent than about his starving tenants. To escape the horrors of the Famine, you make up your mind to travel 3,100 miles (5,000 km) across the Atlantic in the hope of starting a new life with your family. You'll be packed like sardines into a leaky, stinking ship. You must endure seasickness, storms, a vicious crew, rotten food, unsafe water, and worst of all, the deadly "black fever."

CANADA

Grosse Isle

Quebec

During the Famine—also known as the "Great Hunger"—one million Irish emigrants sailed across the Atlantic, while another million died at home from starvation and fever.

GREAT BRITAIN

County Mayo (You live here)

Dublin

IRELAND

Liverpool

New York

USA

Your whole family lives on a small patch of land, growing row after row of potatoes.

Scratching Out a Living

THE WEST COAST
Like most people here, you live off the land. It's hard to grow anything in the rocky, boggy ground. Seaweed improves the soil, but it weighs a ton!

POTATOES. Potatoes are the only crop that's easy to grow in the poor soil where you live. Luckily, they are very nutritious. One in three people in Ireland eat almost nothing but potatoes.

OUT IN THE STICKS. Like most country folk, you've never been more than a few miles from home. Yet many visitors to Ireland notice how kind local people are to passing strangers.

Before the Famine

You spend much of your time working for your landlord. Rents are high—but make sure you pay on time! Your landlord wants an excuse to get rid of you so he can use the land for sheep. Not that you ever see him—he spends most of his time in London, where he is an MP (Member of Parliament).

By the 1840s, Britain, a largely Protestant country, has ruled Ireland, a mainly Catholic country, for 600 years.* The Irish have rebelled many times, but they stand little chance against the British army. After each rebellion, the British grab more land from the Catholic Irish and give it to their Protestant supporters. In the 17th century, the British kicked Catholics off their land in the northern part of Ireland and replaced them with Protestant settlers from Scotland.

*See note on page 30.

Help yourself to potatoes.

Under British law, life is hard for Catholics. Until 1829, most Irish people couldn't buy land, vote, go to church, carry a sword, or own a horse worth over five pounds.

Out of my way, slowpoke!

Handy Hint

That pig you're raising may look delicious, but it's not for eating—selling it will pay a big part of the rent.

HOME, SWEET HOME? Your cottage is an old cowshed. It has no windows, just a hole in the roof to let the smoke out. A fire in the middle of the room keeps you warm. You share your home with chickens, ducks, and a pig.

That rat is after our food.

Just like our landlord!

The Workhouse

One rainy day in August 1845, you notice an awful stench in the air. When you dig up your potatoes, some are healthy, but many are black and slimy. All across Ireland, fields of potatoes are turning into a stinking, rotting mess. A third of the crop is lost. Luckily you have enough potatoes to get through the winter. By the following spring, however, some of your neighbors have already run out of food. They head reluctantly for the dreaded workhouses. Built to house the poor and homeless, workhouses are damp, filthy, and crowded. The food they serve is often rotten, but at least you're not starving.

WHAT'S HAPPENED?
Experts have no idea why the potatoes are rotting. They blame the cold weather, heavy summer rains, insects, and poison in the air. When they finally figure out that a fungus is making the potatoes rot, they're 30 years too late.

What Else Is There to Eat?

NETTLES. Nuts, dandelions, roots, mushrooms, berries, and stinging nettles are all edible, but many can be picked only at certain times of year.

MEAT. Dogs, donkeys, horses, and any wild birds you can catch would make a good meal. If you had a cow you could drain two quarts of blood from it without weakening it much; mix this with vegetables.

FISH. There is little fish to eat, as the tiny boats used by local fishermen are too flimsy to go far from shore. If you lived near the sea you could eat shellfish or seaweed, but they soon run out.

Do you mind if I shut the window?

With what?

TRAPPED! Workhouses are places where the poor are offered food and shelter when they have nowhere else to go. But they are like prisons. Once you enter, you cannot leave. You work all day at boring jobs such as knitting or breaking rocks into stones.

Families are torn apart, as men are forced to live in different buildings from their wives and children. The rules are very strict: there is no answering back. All meals must be eaten in silence.

The Great Hunger

By the summer of 1846, thousands of people in your area are starving. Some villages are already deserted. The British government sets up stores all over Ireland to sell corn, but it's too expensive for poor farmers like you. Crowds gather outside the workhouses, begging for food.

The government starts lending money to landlords, so they can pay poor people to do useful jobs like mending roads. But you wait months while the paperwork is sorted out. Things go from bad to worse. The winter of 1846–47 is bitterly cold. Whole families are found dead in their cottages. In the spring, free soup kitchens are set up outside workhouses. They hand out bowls of "stirabout," a watery soup made from meal, water, and rice.

Soup kitchens will feed your family, but you feel ashamed to be standing in line with a bowl in your hand. Some soup kitchens feed you only if you promise to become a Protestant!

Eat it up, man. It'll do you good.

Will it?

FULL UP! In one workhouse, 150 boys have to share 24 beds. By 1847, people are dying inside the workhouses as they run out of food.

GUILTY! Anyone caught stealing is shipped to Australia. Some are so desperate for food that they commit petty crimes; at least in prison they will be fed.

RIOT. Watching friends and relatives wither away is enough to make you riot, but there are too many British soldiers around.

KEEP TRYING. In 1846 the potato crop is healthy, but you've already had to eat the seed potatoes needed to plant next year's crop.

Handy Hint

If you're lucky enough to get work, beware of "gombeen men" who offer to lend you money while you are waiting to be paid. They'll rip you off!

PRIME MINISTER Robert Peel buys $500,000 worth of maize to send to Ireland. But many British MPs do not want to help – they believe the landlords in Ireland should pay for the emergency food. When help does come, it's too little, too late. By 1847 three million Irish people are starving. Some drop dead as they stand in line at the soup kitchens.

Get Out!

In early 1847, disease breaks out all over Ireland. The hospitals cannot cope, but the British parliament leaves it to the landlords to deal with the problem. Some try to help, but many others kick starving tenants off their land for not paying the rent. Teams of "wreckers" smash down doors with axes, then take cottages apart stone by stone.

Families are forced to live by the roadside. Many die of cold. Some huddle together in shallow holes covered with sticks or turf. That spring, the fungus destroys the potato crop again. When you visit your landlord's agent he offers you tickets to America if you leave your land. You accept: it's your only hope.

That was our home!

Why Go to America?

Next!

DEATH. During the Famine, 1.5 million Irish people die. To cope with the numbers, bodies are buried using "sliding coffins." The bottom of the coffin opens, dropping the body into a large pit. Then the coffin can be used again.

EVICTION. Between 1849 and 1854, some 49,000 families are thrown out of their homes. In Mayo, your county on the west coast, thousands of homeless families die by the side of the road.

Handy Hint

It's dangerous to fight back. Rebels in Tipperary trap the police in a cottage in the middle of widow McCormack's cabbage patch. Fighting goes on for several hours. But when more police arrive, the rebels are forced to flee.

NEWS. You get a letter from your cousin in New York. America sounds wonderful—but he hasn't told you about the people who die on the way over—or struggle to find a job when they arrive.

JAIL. After 1848, anyone who protests can be thrown in jail. Troops are everywhere. The British are afraid of an uprising, but ordinary Irish people are too spread out and weak to rebel.

The Famine Ship

Most ships going to America leave from Dublin, on the east coast of Ireland. Your family must walk hundreds of miles to get there. It could be worse; many people are dying on the road. Others cannot afford to pay for the journey to England, let alone America. Most of your village is emigrating, so at least you'll be with friends.

You arrive in Dublin exhausted but alive. The quays are busy with the sound of horses' hooves and the shouts of dockers unloading cargo. Ticket in hand, you join a line of famine victims that stretches 2 miles (3 km) from the docks. There is little time for tears or farewells; you are herded like cattle onto the ships. You carry a few bags and pots and pans for cooking, but very little else.

SHIPSHAPE? Over five years, 5,000 ships sail across the Atlantic with Irish emigrants. Many are leaky old hulks that have been patched up in a hurry by owners hoping to make a quick buck. The *Elizabeth and Sarah* has been afloat for 83 years!

All Aboard!

HEALTHY? Your whole family must pass a medical examination and get their tickets stamped.

Say 'Ah!'

LATE! If you're late, run to the dock gate, fling your luggage onboard, and jump—hopefully you'll land on deck. A man in a rowboat waits below for anyone who misses!

BAG CHECK. Once the trip is underway, your bags are inspected. Any stowaways are returned to shore.

Handy Hint

If you can't afford a ticket, try to charm your way onboard. In Cork, a sea captain took pity on Patrick Crotty and hired him for the voyage.

BRACE YOURSELF. People are pulled onboard in a heap. Even if you fall flat on your face, the next person is pulled on top of you!

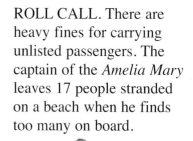

ROLL CALL. There are heavy fines for carrying unlisted passengers. The captain of the *Amelia Mary* leaves 17 people stranded on a beach when he finds too many on board.

15

Bon Voyage

Onboard, you learn that the ship is going to Canada, not New York as you were promised—because it's cheaper to sail to Canada! And the ship is stopping in Liverpool, England. Some passengers are too poor to travel any farther and end up staying there.

After a couple of days, you board the ship again. Several passengers have had their bags stolen. You're given a tiny space to live in. Luckily, you have only three children; there are nine in the family next to you. Not everyone is poor. Some can afford a cabin. The crossing usually takes 40–45 days, but due to storms, one ship, the *Industry*, takes 106 days to reach America, and 17 people starve to death on the way.

RULES. If you break the ship's rules, you risk being beaten by the crew or lashed with rope.

One rule is that you can't wash clothes on a Sunday.

You with the clean shirt— that's 20 lashes!

Life Onboard

THE CAPTAIN'S WORD is law. If passengers complain, they can be charged with mutiny—punishable by hanging!

Handy Hint

It's easy to get bored onboard. Dancing and singing help to keep spirits up, but as the voyage goes on, you may not have the strength for this.

STOWAWAYS. If stowaways appear once the ship is out to sea, some captains refuse to give them rations. To stay alive, they'll have to beg food from the other passengers.

HOLD YOUR NOSE! Most of the time passengers are kept below decks. The only place to pour your waste is into the hold below. The smell makes it hard to breathe. The sailors are supposed to do the cleaning, but often leave it to passengers.

What have we here, then?

SLEEP TIGHT! On the *Elizabeth and Sarah*, most of the wooden bunks collapse soon after the ship sets off. Passengers have to sleep on the floor.

Staying Alive

Y ou're allowed on deck to cook your meals using fire boxes—wooden boxes lined with bricks. Often there isn't enough fuel to cook your food properly, but any food is welcome after the horrors of the Famine. Each week you are supposed to get 7 pounds (3 kg) of bread, crackers, flour, rice, oatmeal, and potatoes, but on your ship people get only half this amount. You can earn more food by working as a crew member, but you'll get beaten if you make a mistake. Each day you also get a gallon (5 l) of water. You must line up behind a white line, and if you cross it by mistake, you lose your ration.

FIRE! Cooking on deck is risky: 9,000 emigrants die from onboard fires. If you are forced to abandon ship, there are few if any lifeboats. When the *Ocean Monarch* catches fire just 25 miles (40 km) from Liverpool, 170 passengers die.

HARD CHEESE. On some ships the only rations are moldy crackers. Cross your fingers and hope that some of the passengers know how to catch fish when you get near the Canadian coast.

STEALING. Forget it! Thieves are flayed with a whip known as the cat-o'-nine-tails. On one ship, when passengers try to break into the food storeroom, the captain threatens them with a musket.

ORDER. Fights can break out between violent passengers. On most ships the passengers elect a committee to make up rules and settle arguments.

Handy Hint

Some rules do make sense. Don't smoke below decks—some ships are carrying gunpowder for the British government!

FIRE SAFETY.
At the end of the set meal times, a cabin boy nicknamed "Jack in the Shrouds" puts out fires by pouring water on the fire boxes below.

Couldn't you wait till it's cooked?

Stormy Weather

The wind is one of your only friends, speeding you to Canada, but it can also be your greatest enemy. During a storm, the hatches are shut and passengers are trapped down below, sometimes in complete darkness. You cling tightly to your children to keep them from being flung about. It's terrifying. Storm winds can blow a ship off course or force it to turn back. They also force the crew to lower the sails, slowing down the ship. In 1848 the *Creole* limps back into Cork after spending three weeks at sea. It has lost most of its sails and two masts after being struck by lightning.

Keeping Your Head in a Storm

TOSSED ABOUT. During a storm, anything not tied down gets thrown from one side to the other: people, boxes, barrels, and even dead bodies, all in one big heap.

GET ON TOP. Make sure you're in the top bunk. It's not much fun if the people above you are seasick.

LEAK! Many famine ships are leaky old tubs that let in lots of water during a storm. Pray that the ship doesn't break up!

Should we have stayed at home?

Handy Hint

Avoid a winter crossing if you can —that's the time of the worst storms. The short days and long nights make the voyage even more depressing.

I can't stay like this till we get to Canada...

IN A FIX. As the ship rolls about, gaps open and close between the planks. These can trap passengers' clothing, especially women's skirts. You could be pinned down for hours.

SQUASHED. In a bad storm, the captain of the *Londonderry* forces all 174 passengers into a small cabin; 72 people are crushed or suffocated.

SWEPT AWAY. If you do make it up onto the deck, there's a good chance you'll be swept away by the waves.

Iceberg!

After several days of stormy weather, the hatches are opened and passengers can go on deck in small groups. It's good to get away from the terrible stench below. Some of the children play catch on deck. But the danger isn't over yet—you could still be shipwrecked!

On a clear day, icebergs can be spotted through a telescope—but not in thick fog. During the five Famine years (1845–49), 50 ships sink after hitting icebergs or rocks. Icebergs can be more than two-thirds of a mile (1 km) long and 200 feet (60 m) high. It's one more hazard for poor emigrants on their way to a new life.

On the Lookout!

WHALES are seen as a sign of bad luck by the crew. Dolphins and flying fish are also common sights on Atlantic crossings. Sharks often follow ships in the hope of finding a tasty morsel…

SLOBS are slimy objects that float in the water. Some look like a lemon cut in half. You may also see jellyfish or Portuguese man-of-wars.

LIQUID FIRE. At night, tiny luminous creatures in the water make the ship look as if it is gliding on liquid fire—though only passengers who can afford cabins can see this.

GOING AGROUND. In 1850 the *Constitution* sailing from Belfast runs aground just after sighting land. Luckily, passengers escape to shore using a web of ropes.

Handy Hint

When you're up on deck it's worth scanning the horizon. A flock of birds is a good sign that land is near. Hooray!

You don't usually see them this far north.

When the Hannah strikes an iceberg the sailors jump into a lifeboat, leaving the passengers to die. But the ship takes 40 minutes to sink, giving the passengers time to climb onto the iceberg. They huddle together for 15 hours, some wearing only their nightshirts, until another ship comes to the rescue. Though 129 people are saved, many freeze to death and others are crushed by the shifting ice.

The "Coffin Ships"

Y ou're just beginning to enjoy a spell of good weather when there's trouble onboard. One of the passengers has died of fever, and in the cramped spaces below deck it spreads like wildfire.

Being shut up in the dark with fever victims makes some passengers panic. The terrible moans of sick people keep you awake all night.

Many emigrants are still weak from the lack of food and cannot fight the fever. Children and the elderly are most at risk. It is heartbreaking to see people dying so close to the shores of Canada.

OVERBOARD. The fever can affect people's minds. Some victims jump off the ship in a frenzy.

No Escape!

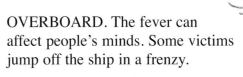
Are we there yet?

Yecch!!

SKELETON CREW!
The crew of the *Looshtauk* goes down with fever. Only the captain and first mate are healthy enough to sail the ship, with help from passengers.

WIPED OUT. When the *Virginius* arrives in America, 158 people have died since leaving Ireland and another 106 are ill with fever. Only eight people onboard are still healthy at the end of the voyage.

DIRTY WATER. The fever isn't helped by the fact that after several weeks at sea, the drinking water turns bad and isn't safe to drink.

Handy Hint

If you have any money left, try to bribe the steward for some extra food for your children.
It could be the difference between life and death.

There are several deaths every day. Bodies are wrapped in sailcloth and thrown overboard. Out of 4,500 passengers who were headed to Montreal, Canada, in July 1847, more than 800 have died on the way and another 800 are sick with fever. No wonder people call these boats "coffin ships."

The Island of Death

The sight of other ships means the coast is near. Your ship must now safely navigate upriver to reach port. The next day the fog clears. Everyone who can rushes on deck. There's land on both sides! But your hopes are soon dashed. Because of the fever, all passengers must now pass a medical inspection before being ferried to Quebec. Another 20 vessels are lined up along the river, all waiting their turn. The inspection takes place on Grosse Isle, a rocky island just 3 miles (5 km) long and a mile (1.5 km) wide. Its hospital is unable to cope. After a few weeks, hordes of emigrants are sent inland, taking the fever with them. By a miracle, everyone in your family is still alive.

The Horrors of Grosse Isle

FLOATING CORPSES. Most ships are full of the ill and the dying. Many ships dump bodies overboard.

NO AMBULANCE. There is a stream of small boats carrying emigrants to shore. The sick are flung onto the beach. Many crawl up to the hospital—if they can.

FULL UP. Within two weeks of your arrival, there are 850 patients in the tiny hospital, 500 more ill with fever, and 13,000 waiting on ships to be examined. Tents are hastily put up, but proper quarantine is impossible. The sick and the healthy are put together and the fever spreads again. If you survive, you'll never forget the moans of the dying.

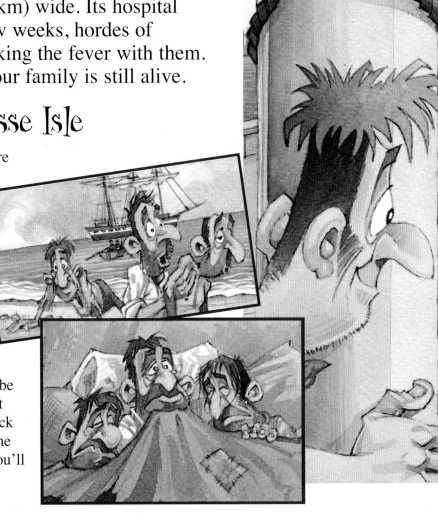

Emigrants cheer at the sight of land—but for many the first two weeks in Canada turn into a nightmare. Around 7,000 are buried at Grosse Isle.

Handy Hint

Don't be fooled if people suffering from fever suddenly seem to cheer up and start chatting. Sadly, that is usually a sign that they are about to die.

We've made it!

New York

YOU'VE LANDED in Canada, but almost half of all Irish emigrants sail to New York—during the Famine years more than 650,000 arrive on 2,743 voyages. These people usually fare better than those sailing to Canada. There are stricter rules for U.S. ships, and passengers are fed better.

Journey's End

Quebec was originally a French colony, so there are few jobs for people who don't speak French. So, like most Irish emigrants, you head south for the United States. It's a long journey on foot. By the time you arrive in New York, you're exhausted. But America is a good place to be if you can work with your hands. Your wife gets a job as a servant in a rich home, and you become one of many Irishmen working on the railroads. You will never forget the Famine or the coffin ships, but you and your family have survived the hunger and fever to build a new life America.

COLD. At least your family traveled in summer—15,000 emigrants will freeze to death while journeying through the harsh North American winter.

Keep Your Wits About You!

EASY PICKINGS. The docks are swarming with "runners." Some wear bright green waistcoats to attract Irish emigrants. They will either steal your luggage or carry it to a boarding house and demand an outrageous fee.

TRULY AWFUL. Some runners sell fake railroad tickets across the United States. When one man refuses to buy a ticket from "Awful" Gardner, Gardner breaks his jaw!

N.I.N.A. Irish emigrants are not always welcome: they are often poor, and many carry the fever with them. Many job advertisements say, "No Irish Need Apply."

TOUGH WORK. Many emigrants fall ill because they start work while they are still weak from the crossing. Others are forced to accept dangerous jobs, such as laying explosives to blast a path for railroads.

Handy Hint

Try not to look too tough! Irish emigrants are often picked on by crime bosses and forced to join violent gangs.

Come on, lazybones. What's your excuse?

Poverty, repression, famine, fever, coffin ships, exhaustion...

The Irish in America

By 1850 there were more Irish in New York than in Dublin, the capital of Ireland. Today, some 44 million Americans are of Irish heritage.

Car maker Henry Ford was a direct descendant of a Famine emigrant. Presidents John F. Kennedy, Richard Nixon, Ronald Reagan, and George W. Bush all had Irish ancestors, as did pioneer Daniel Boone, playwright Eugene O'Neill, and film star John Wayne.

John F. Kennedy

Ronald Reagan

George W. Bush

Glossary

Note: Ireland, Britain, and England
During the period described in this book—in fact, from 1801 to 1922—Ireland, England, Scotland, and Wales were all part of the United Kingdom of Great Britain and Ireland. The whole kingdom was ruled by the British government in London, England. But the English had been fighting over Ireland since the middle ages—long before Great Britain was formed in 1707. Most of the island of Ireland became a separate country in 1922 (it has been the Republic of Ireland since 1949), but today, Northern Ireland is still part of the U.K.

evict To force someone to leave their home, legally or illegally.

fever A name that is sometimes given to any kind of illness in which a high temperature is one of the symptoms.

first mate The second-in-command on a merchant ship.

gombeen man An Irish term for a moneylender or shopkeeper who sells goods to poor people on credit and then charges them a very high rate of interest.

Portuguese man-of-war A sea creature which resembles a jellyfish, but is really a group of separate animals living together. It has a very painful sting.

quay (pronounced like "key") A platform next to the water where ships are loaded and unloaded.

seed potatoes Potatoes that are not eaten, but saved and planted to grow next year's crop.

shrouds Part of the rigging of a sailing ship; a series of ropes that help to brace the mast, with smaller ropes tied across them to make a sort of ladder for the crew.

sliding coffin A coffin with a removable bottom, so that a body can be dropped from it into the grave, and the same coffin can then be used again for other bodies.

workhouse A place where poor people were housed and fed at public expense. In return, they were required to do simple physical work.

Index